Special Acknowledgements

To all Librarians, for their help and guidance.

To both Sister M. Helen Scicchitano and Sister M. Assumption for their translation into Latin of the story; "Faint Fragrance".

To my one time enemy in the Far East for the event of "In The Cross Hairs."

To US Army Garrison at Fort Indiantown Gap for "Children Are Children."

To All Mothers for "Mother Take Care."

To the coal crackers of Pennsylvania for "Old Howard."

To the opposite sex for lyrics & One Little Flower.

To "Someone" . . . for "I Just had A Chat With."

To Man for "Oh, Man."

To Mary and Marion for illustrations.

<u>Notes</u>

No Time To Read During Lunch?

Try The Next Few Minutes.

CONTENTS:

Faint Fragrance
Una Fragranza
One Little Flower
Children Are Children
My Dream Girl
The Speed Bumps Of Life
In The Cross Hairs
Share What's In Your Heart
I Just Had A Chat With
Old Howard
Oh, Man

"FAINT FRAGRANCE"

The fragrance of balanced, blended, and correctly mixed aromas fill ones nostrils under varied circumstances. Flowers at weddings, get well baskets where the contents overcome the antiseptic hue of the sick area, and yes, even at a wake, the heartiness is there.

The refreshing scent of unexplainable, unidentifiable origin, as after the summer storm, the early morning hours, and even after an all night snow . . . The fragrance is there! Where is it from? Quite possibly the following could be one answer.

When the wise men came to adore Christ, among their assorted gifts of oils and varied items with fragrances, the men were astounded at the already faint presence of what they accepted as Heavenly. The aroma of purity, caring, and love surrounding our newborn king.

Throughout the years, this delightful and refreshing fragrance persists and was repeatedly rejuvenated during certain events during our Lord's stay of about thirty years on earth with us.

Men have not been able to explain or understand the how, why, or where, they can only speculate. Yet when purity, sincere caring, and love are extended, the fragrance is there, faint . . . but always there.

When John the Baptist conducted his baptism, it was there and became greater as the dove of the Holy Spirit descended from heaven on Christ. The fragrance was pleasant, refreshingly clean, natural purity with caring and love as a blend.

The gathering of disciples, the many sermons either on a hillside or in a synagogue, this same refreshing fragrance . . . purity, caring, and love.

On board ship, walking on the sea, calming that same sea, visiting in a prison, healing in a bedroom or on a sidewalk, the same faint but very, very noticeable fragrance . . . purity, caring and love.

Having to chastise Judas for objecting to the oil that Mary Magdalene has placed on Jesus, even on his beard. - Judas thought the money she had paid for it would have been better

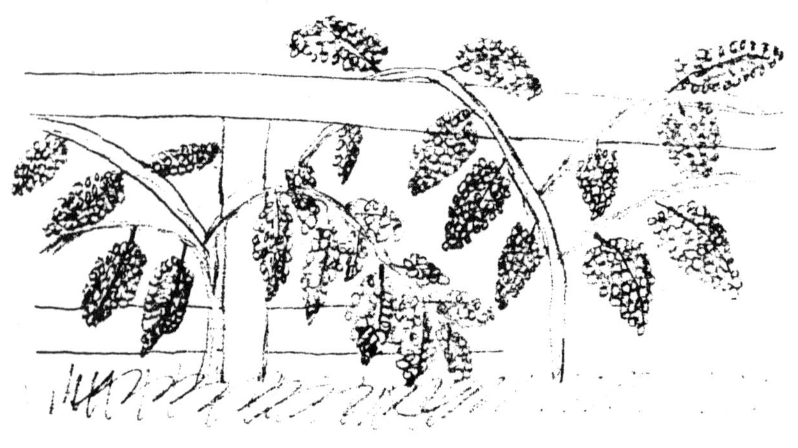

spent on the poor - Christ answered truthfully, "the poor you have with you always; I will be with you but a short time." Purity, with caring and love, as the fragrance is reinstalled."

Shortly thereafter, the betrayers and even his captors sensed it, a faint but noticeable fragrance . . . but their interest is elsewhere. Standing before Pilate, His accusers, His mockers - during the condemnation - all near Him sense a faint but noticeable fragrance . . . purity, caring and love. The torturous walk through the streets, falling as the heavy cross took its toll of His strength; and as the stranger who would help Christ carry the cross to the top of Golgotha; sensed in His nostrils the faint fragrance of purity, caring, and love.

The guards in disrobing and nailing Him are overwhelmed by the faint fragrance of purity, caring and love. Raging rain protesting what has been done, with flashes of lightning aiding in the circulation of the fragrance of purity, caring, and love. Someone within the ranks of the guard force exclaimed, "Surely this is the Son of God."

When the women visited and found an empty tomb, there was something very recognizable to them. The faint frangrance of purity, caring, and love. As Jesus left the earth to ascend to the Father, all who were there knew the faint fragrance of purity, caring, and love.

Now in our generation; I am quite sure with all our learning and understanding; when unexplained things cross our paths, why not take a moment . . . close your eyes . . . inhale slowly . . . bet you get a faint fragrance of purity, caring and love. As for me, I sense a soft tint of grape arbor aroma.

UNA FRAGRANZA

La fragranza bilancia mistura e' correttamente mescolare aroma riempire i mostrile sotto varie circumstance. Fiori di Matrimonio, basketti per stare bene, che coprano' il odore anticeptico della stanza di ammalate. Si anche dove sono gli morte la fraganza e li. La rinfrescante profumo incomprehencile di origine' come dopo il burasco d'estate, la matina presto, il burasco d'estate, e neve dopo la notte, la fragansa e' ancora li.

Quando hanno venuto le tre uomini sapiente a adorare Christo, insieme alle loro regali di assortamente di olio e varie profumi, erano stupefato alla presenza della celeste aroma di purita, cura, e amore che cera intorno al il nuovo nato Re.

Durante' gli anni, questo delizioso e rinfrescato fragraza persisteva, e stato rejuvenato durante tanto momente durante trenta tre anni che il Signore e stato con noi sulla terra.

Uomini non possono comprendere come mai o perche. Solo possano speculare, pero' quando la purita' sincere e l'amore sono prolungato, la fraganza e li, debole ma sempre li. Quando Giovane Baptista batisava era li, perche lo Spirito Santo veniva dal cielo sopra "Christo." La fraganza era pulito, purita naturale, con aura, e amore mistura. Sulla nave, camminare sul acqua, calmare l'acqua, visitare prigione, curare ammalate nella stanza o sopra pavimento, cera sempre questo fraganza di amore e servizio. Gesu doveva rimprovere Juda perche non voleva che Maria Madalena usava l'olio. Credeva invece che doveva dare il denaro ai poveri. Il Signore ha risposto i poveri abbiam sempre con noi. Io saro con loro pocco tempo - purita, cura, amore. In pocco tempo dopo anche le sui inemeci sentivano una debole perfumo ma non erano interesate. Davanti a Pilato le sui accusatori, e durante la dondemazione tutti vicie sensano una debole legere fraganza di purita, cura, amore. La Tomentato camminato nella strada, candento sotto la croce pesanto ha culminato suo forza, e come il straniero che auitera' Christo portare la croce in cima di Gogatha sense nel nostrile la debole fraganza di puita, aira, amore gli custodi nel spogliare (dinuclare) e' mettendo i

chiodi sensivano nelle lori nostrile la fraganza di purita, cuara, amore. Piogia, tempesta, protestazione quello che hanno fatto lampi. Aiutano la circulazione della fraganza di purita, cura, amore. Qualcuno esclama "Sicuro questo e il Figlio di Dio."

Quando le donne hanno visitato la tomba hanna conosicuto suluto la fraganza di purita, cura, e amore.

Quando il signore la lasciato questa terra per andare al Padre tutti spaevano la fraganza di purita, cua, amore. Adesso nella nostra generazione sono sicuro con tutto la nostra sapienza, quando tribulazione vangano chudi gli occhi, respira, adaggio. Io scommessa che aura una fraganza di purita cura amore. A me, senso un gentile tinta di uva e pergiato'.

ONE LITTLE FLOWER

A flower, resting in an unattended holder,
Nearing the wilting stage.
Suddenly springs back to radiant life,
When placed into the hand of any person wanting.
If we should look further down the roadway,
Scanning faces in the crowd.
Some showing sadness and dismay.
What a blessing, if someone,
Handed each a little flower.
Igniting radiance and understanding . . .
They are loved.

CHILDREN ARE CHILDREN

Preface: Who knows if animals talk? . . . They must have some form of communication for them to do just what they do; Exist.

Let us use our imagination for a little while and if we are real quiet, their goings on in and around the den can be tuned into . . . Shhhh . . . listen . . .

"Where are the children?", asked father returning from his daily run to the creek in search for food and other tidbits.

Mother looks up from her knitting and responds, "It would not be a surprise if they are running the path to the water pipe, going across the mountain."

Fathers hair bristles as he goes toward the doorway, "Mother beaver, you know full well I have said over and over, no running the path without someone watching out for the falcon; not to mention the human who drives by our home on his way to the check points on his security patrol; some humans are good, while others are just as bad as the killer birds.

"Father beaver, you must talk to the children.

"Bridget, Judith, Monroe, Donald and Joseph, stop that silly running and hollering, they can hear you all over the area. Remember, we are at an Army Post and living within the confines of an ammunition dump. If the killer birds do not hear you, the humans sure can. Come home at once!"

The children respond quickly. They well know how grumpy father can be when he is angry.

Inside the den, Father asks, "Who came up with the idea of playing on the path to the water pipe?"

Monroe looks at Donald, who in turn looks at Bridget, then Judith and all remaining eyes turn toward Joseph.

"Hah," says Father, "the ring leader?"

Joseph hangs his furry little head and in a low but firm voice tells them, "He had formed a plan, by watching the birds dive and how they swoop low in order to pick up their prey and also the habits of some of the bad humans and he wants to bring all this to a stop."

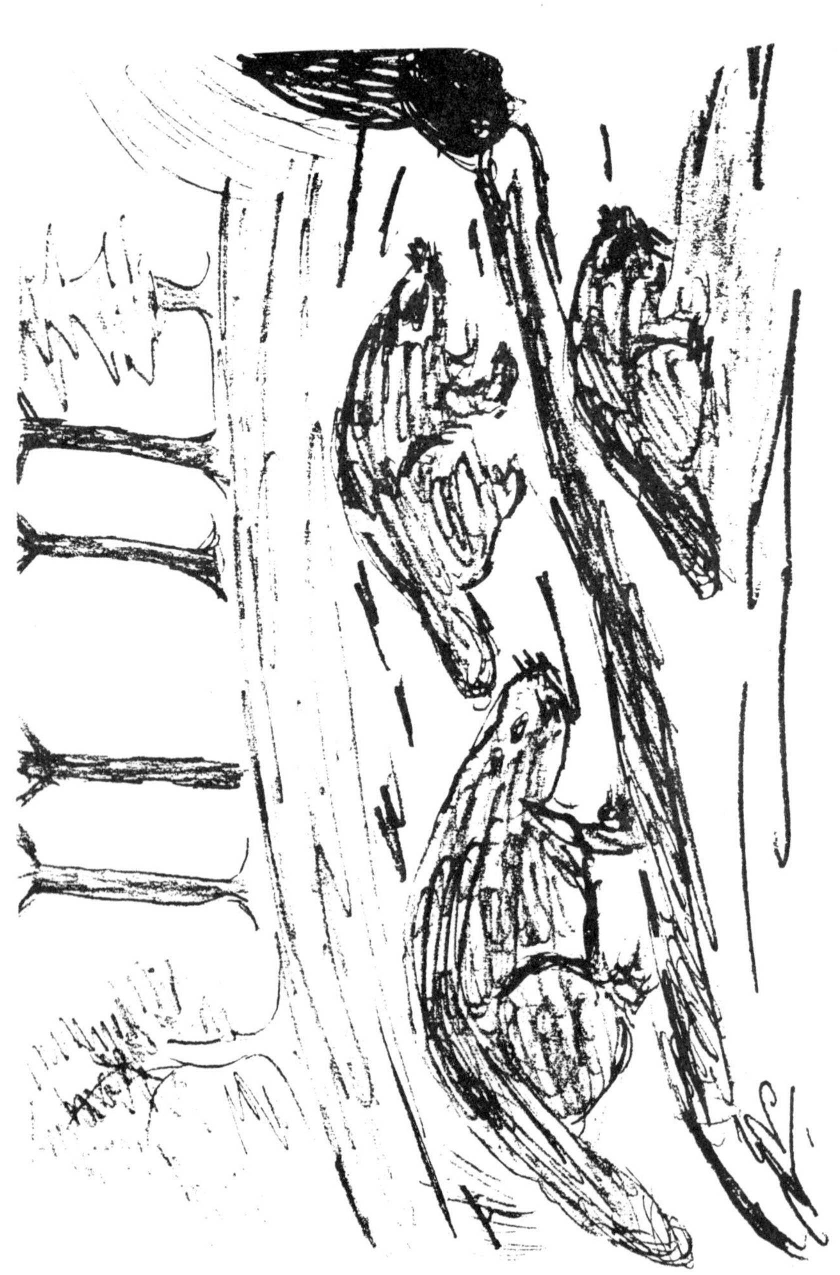

Everyone chuckles, how was a little beaver like Joseph going to do battle with the large birds, let alone humans? Bridget and Donald were laughing so loud, that Mother kept shushing them over and over until they stopped.

Father says, "gather around now children and nestle close and as we gather around the fire, I want to tell you what has happened in the past to some of your brothers and sisters and cousins, when they were at play on the path to the water pipe. "They, like us, love to run and have fun, sometimes without any danger. Then one day as they were on the path, a killer bird swooped down, picked up the one in front, and as it climbed into the air, the screams could be heard when those talons dug in and death came slowly, but surely . . .

Father pauses, sighs and wipes his tears, his voice breaks "another time", he begins, "the vehicle with the large wheels ran over one of the children, never stopping, the bad human could be heard laughing as he drove away."

"So children, do not play on the path to the water pipe and whatever you do, refrain from playing on the roadway of the vehicles . . .

Father looks at Joseph, "Do you fully understand?"

Joseph nods his head in accord.

A period of time went by and one day as Joseph was coming out the den, from habit, he looks up and observed a falcon doing a slow spiral over the den. He knows his plan is a good one, yet should he miscalculate, one of his brothers or sisters may pay a high price for his idea . . . What should he do?

Once again the children are back to the same run, down the path and each time extending their run, foot by foot without regard for safety.

This time Joseph warns them, "Father will really be furious with us if we keep ignoring his warnings!"

The children respond, "You watch for the human or the killer bird and we will watch for you, so you can play also." Scared, Joseph agrees, but really half watches, after all, it is a little cloudy. The killer bird will not fly when it is like this.

He watches and watches until his eyes catch something coming up the road leaving a dust trail. It is the security vehicle with the human and also now on high above is a figure that is starting its slow spiral. Joseph yells, "The killer bird . . . look out! Get off the path". "No, not on the road Judith." The falcon starts its descent, it has targeted Donald or Monroe. "Judith, Bridget don't go on the road." The vehicle is now in a slow turn on the curve toward where the children are. "Get back off the road." The sisters listen and dart back on to the pathway. The falcon is lower and aiming for Monroe and Joseph must now make his move.

The razor sharp talons are in position for the pick up of Monroe and Joseph screams as loud as he can and the falcon responds to the scream as in a desperate lunge, Joseph bumps the talons, the falcon misjudges the opening to the tunnel of the water pipe and crashes into a small hole with a loud ka-plup, breaking its neck and Joseph being so close, jumps to his right and lands on the road, as the vehicle hits him. He thinks of so many good things that have happened to him in his young short life, he hardly feels the bump as he blacks out.

Coming to, Joseph realizes he is being held by the human and he is sure this is it! Humans are bad! But this one is smiling and looking at him. "Little guy, I would have shot that glutton bird, because he just killed for the sake of it, however, I would have been dismissed for firing my weapon, so my friend, you did us both a service." The human slowly checked each one of Joseph's paws and runs his hand over his tummy and back, then says, "Little guy, you're in good shape," and very tenderly places Joseph off the roadway, closest to the pathway that will take him home. As they part, it appears that each one of them has a tear in their eye as the human waves goodbye.

Things are different at home now, we all listen and do our best to watch where we play and also watch each other. Sometimes we see the good human that helped our Joseph.

Animals talk? You say hah! But then again if not, who wrote this tale?

MY DREAM GIRL

What is a dream?
With scene after scene.
And you, in the center of it all.
I think it's just great,
As the village bells chime.
On our very next date,
You will be mine
Your my dream girl,
Your sweet as can be.
My scheme girl,
Building things with me.
I can't wait, until the night is here.
I can't wait, until I hold you near.
Now day is dawning,
We will soon be apart.
With each parting,
A tear fills my heart.
Yet I'll go right on dreaming,
And hoping as before.
You will be my dream girl, Forever more.
Oh, yes my dream girl . . . Forever more.

THE SPEED BUMPS OF LIFE

Somehow it seems most mothers,
Share the thought: They have been blessed.
Watching their children grow taller,
Knowing soon. . . They must leave the nest.

Oh, Mother take care,
Oh, Mother beware.
The speed bumps of life,
Are sometimes unfair.

First date, home a bit late,
As innocence beams from their eyes.
Full well knowing, promises spoken,
In a short space of time, will surely be broken.

Oh, Mother take care,
Oh, Mother beware.
The speed bumps of life,
Are sometimes unfair.

The years pass by, and she sits alone.
Leafing through the album of memory,

Puppies and kittens, who lost this mitten?
Ring echoes of a completely filled home.
But as each page of life quickly ages,
All too soon, each one becomes history.

Oh, Mother take care,
Oh, Mother beware.
The speed bumps of life,
Are sometimes unfair.

IN THE CROSS HAIRS

As a young boy, showing respect for others had top priority in my family. My maturity in no way diminished this feeling, yet when I found myself a professional soldier and a leader of troops against an enemy, I had to rethink my priorities.

I had to remember, this son of a bitch would kill me if he got the chance, and he would not hesitate to kill my troops should the opportunity exist.

In battle, the only item between the enemy and myself, was my MIC sniper rifle with scope. I am an infantry soldier (grunt) with a good killing instrument. And for the record, no wincing or hesitation to take any of them out, interfered with my judgement. Yet some questions surface and must be answered.

In war, is it necessary to kill just for the sake of killing? Do I spare the life of a dedicated enemy? Do I kill to avoid being killed or to save someone else from being killed?

I encountered a situation where all of the above came into focus, and to this day, I ask myself, when I had an enemy dead center in my scope cross hairs, did I do the right thing?

On the battlefield, in a stagnant situation, we establish what is known as a Listening Post (LP), or an Out Post (OP), even a Forward Position (FP). This placement is well in front of the front line as we know it or using military talk, The Main Line of Resistance (MLR). The purpose of each is self explanatory . . . Listen . . . Observe . . . Report any activity or actions of the enemy in front of the battle line.

To the left of our LP, was a small placement of sand bags, built to just about hip height, to allow a man to stand and observe all events to his front, left and right.

All travel was either up the finger or down the finger of the hill we were located on.

The communications between the Command Post on top of the hill consisted of a field telephone connected to field wire which we called a land line, as all one had to do, was twist the

crank along side the phone box and then move a small butter-fly control on the hand piece to talk or whisper to the person assigned to handle all transmissions.

Over a short period of time, all movements, up the hill or down became routine. Wait for darkness, then have two or three troops move out and down the finger of the hill to occupy the LP. Each time this was accomplished, most times the troops were leary of the possibility that the enemy could have moved earlier and prepared an ambush for our team. Constant monitoring by select troops on line reduced this confrontation from taking place, by striking at the enemy should they be headed toward the LP.

It hardly seems possible, that under hostile conditions, anyone friendly or enemy, would become so complacent, as to disregard one's own safety, but that is exactly what happens, up until an event takes place to then return all players to reality, where once again the professional soldier resurfaces.

My troops had occupied the LP for a few hours and I decided to accompany the relief team in order to check the position and chat with the troops. Besides, there had been some reports of enemy movement in front of our adjoining units, giving the possibility of enemy contact.

Standing inside the LP, at the left corner, I was comparing the very cold, clear moonlit night. A glance upward through the wire mesh allowed me to see a star filled dark sky to my direct front. As I am scanning from right to left, I am frozen in motion by a movement of a figure that is slowly rising taller and taller just behind one of our Korean soldiers manning the little revetment to the left of the LP. There was sufficient moonlight to give a clear picture of what we now had shaping up. The figure was a large Chinese marine and he positioned himself to the rear of my Korean, known to us as J. W. Yeh. There was no way to forewarn him of what was taking place and I slowly pressed closer to the wall and eased my MIC sniper rifle barrel out through the chicken wire and allowed it to rest on the wire forming a hole. We had put the wire there in order to stop or bounce back, toward the thrower of any type

grenade, hurled at the LP.

As I scoped in with my cross hairs directly between the eye brows of the Chinese Troop, I whispered for the other man in the LP to call the CP and let them know what was going on. Do all troops know of Murphy's Law? You bet, communications were out and they were checking out the problem, meaning sooner or later, someone was going to come down the hill and startle this enemy. Someone was going to get hurt, if not killed.

My decision at the moment, kill him now. Next thing I start to rationalize, he has nothing in his hands . . . kill the son of a bitch my training demands. He now starts to slowly inch his way closer to Yeh, what an easy target this big bastard is. My trigger finger starts taking up the slack on the trigger, there is no wavering in my sight picture, as the barrel is resting on a steady surface. Once again the thought, he has done nothing wrong except try his luck at seeing how close he can get to Yeh, nothing to warrant a bullet. This overgrown boob has either balls or no sense! I prefer to think of it as no sense. Kill him echoes my instinct, screw him, he is the enemy . . . the men will think more of you if I take him out. No, I can still see plainly his outline and both arms are relaxed with nothing in his hands.

Yeh leans forward and rests his hands on the top row of sandbags, looking straight ahead. I have reached the point of no more slack on the trigger, breathe, aim, squeeze and sight, BASS. How ironic, such a simple basic training class comes to mind. Kill him before he hurts Yeh. I pray a hasty prayer, "Lord, I do not want to kill just to kill, yet I must protect my soldier, as I would want him to cover me. If this enemy does not attempt to harm Yeh, I will not harm him either. Help me do the right thing." I have no knowledge if the Chinese may have detected a glint of my rifle barrel and after what I thought was an awful long time, the Chinese soldier raises both hands in an upward position to shoulder height and slowly moves back and down the finger of the hill. I release pressure on the trigger and go out to Yeh and as I approach him,

he tells me, "Ok, No Chineeseu, No Chineeseu."

Just then to our direct front, there is much small arms fire, one of our patrols have engaged the enemy. Soon the firing stops and after a short while, our troops come past the LP on their way back to the top of the hill. I asked the patrol leader if they got anything, and his reply was, we saw a couple big gooks going north, fired directly at the biggest one. Do not know how we could have missed the big son of a bitch, must have a charmed ass.

I never said a word, only had a question go through my mind, was this the man who was once in the cross hairs? My cross hairs?

There have been many situations that I found myself involved with, that have led me to believe, spare a life and yours may be prolonged? I refer to mortar rounds falling, others hit, and yet I was spared? Fire fights, others wounded, I was spared? But then again, this will be for other stories, such as this one. Ok? Ok.

SHARE WHAT'S IN YOUR HEART

So much time is spent in silence,
Keeping all within your heart.
Hopes and dreams, happy ending scenes.
Why not share what's in your heart.

How do you say you love her?
Can't she tell how much you care?
As you gaze deep in her eyes.
It's so simple my friend, go on tell her.
Why not share what's in your heart.

Those little things she does,
That mean so much to you.
The way she smiles and says hello,
then she asks, how are you? as she whispers
In your ear,
Now's the time to tell her..you love her.
Why not share what's in your heart.

Try not to be the tough guy,
Show her you have tenderness.
Caress and gently hold her,
Share in her happiness.
Then tell her you love her,
Just share what's in your heart..Yes,
Why not share what's in your heart.

I JUST HAD A CHAT WITH

Some years ago, while I was walking across an avenue in Dallas, Texas, enroute to an appointment, my thoughts somehow honed in on the Lord.

I was feeling so grateful for what he had done for me, that seemingly, traffic, pedestrians and surrounding vehicles just vanished. No doubt, in the real world, such happenings are for the movies, but it did occur.

The closer I came to the curbing, the more was my intent and thoughts of many good things that had come my way. People, situations, close calls in battle, sort of my analogy of nice events in my life and as I stepped on the curb, then onto the pavement glancing to my right, there was a person that said to me, "He is sure wonderful, isn't he?" My instant reply, "Yes sir, He sure is."

Turning my head to my front, to be sure that the building I was going to enter was the correct one, then looking back, my friendly person was gone.

I will never forget what he looked like, about five foot ten, clear pink rosy complexion and extremly neat. White hair, styled similar to that worn by Roman senators, in that time period. Large pleasant eyes, deep blue, with a very friendly smile.

As for the type clothing he wore, I am at a loss, my desire is to share with you a fleeting moment in my life when, I just had a chat with. . .

OLD HOWARD

Over the years, I have heard stories and yarns as a youngster, sometimes I was present in their telling, once in awhile, they were handed down to me in a "Can you keep a secret?" style. What you are about to read is a story handed down to me by my grandmother, and who in their wildest imagination would ever think of a grandmother who might fib? . . .

In the coal mining villages of Northeast Pennsylvania, the work is very hard, the hours long, and the pay not really the greatest, so the luxuries of life were either none at all, once in awhile, or a person could ignore his responsibilities and do his own thing. This story deals with an individual who decided to do what he wanted, no matter, what the consequence, even if it meant his family suffered as a result of his gambling and drinking.

For the sake of confidentiality, we'll call this miner, the main character of our story, Jack. His wife was Susan. Their final crisis came after Jack lost his pay and Susan insisted he stop his waywardness or leave, Jack became furious; and after a down and out domestic quarrel with broken dishes, ruined furniture, ruined and severely ill feelings, that no doubt hurt both them and the children, Jack left the house. Susan promptly called Old Howard and reminded him of his offer of a remedy that would stop Jack from his gambling and drinking. She agreed to Howard's help, only if he could assure her that Jack would not be harmed! Old Howard assured her that no harm would come to Jack, only a change, if that was all right with her? So Susan agreed.

The village's strangest person, Old Howard, was rumored to be connected to the Mafia or some other kind of secret organization. He always had funds to help other families with their problems. An aura of mystery surrounded Old Howard. For some strange reason, after people got his aid, most times everything worked out for the better.

Within a two hour span of Susan's and Old Howard's fateful meeting, Jack's youngest boy took so ill he had to go to the hospital. The boy survived, but the recovery period would be long and expensive, and did they have insurance?

On the way home, Jack and Susan discussed what to do; they had no insurance, a limited income; just how in the world were they to handle this? When they arrived home, Old Howard was on the porch swing. "How is it going?" he asked. Susan told him about their son's tragedy before going in to check on the other children. Jack sat down to tell Old Howard about their financial woes and Old Howard responded in the oddest way. "Jack, tonight there will be a large game at the hall; possibly enough to help with all your problems."

Quickly Jack let Old Howard know, "I can't get enough to play the big ones, like tonight's.

Old Howard responded, I'll stake you, but with a promise. Should you win, you'll never gamble or drink again."

Jack thought to himself, "Who the hell is he to tell me what to do or not do?"

Old Howard lit up his worn battered pipe and the aroma of the tobacco took Jack's breath away, "It smells of stinky toe jams." Old Howard agrees smiling, then asks, "What's you want to do, boy?"

OK, it's a deal, now I suppose you want it in writing?"

No, your word is good enough for me. Drive me home and I'll give you the funds. Also, I only want returned what I give you, that understood?

"Yes".

Jack took Old Howard home, got the money and headed for the hall.

It started to snow as Jack entered the hall. Welcomed back as always, he was offered a seat in the on-going game. When he had left before, there were four players, now six were play-ing.

"Are you sure there is a seat for me?" Jack asked. As he sat down, two strangers, one on his left and one on his right, took Jack in. The one to Jack's right said, "We can always use your money." Most of the others laughed along with Jack.

"Well maybe I can use yours", Jack replied and as he looked into the stranger's eyes, for a moment a cold chill of fear tin-gled in his body. The cold dark unsmiling stare of the stranger

seemed an eternity of eye to eye contact. Jack thought to himself, hard to read what kind of hand this fella may be holding!

The men at the table asked the stranger where they were headed and where they were from? The one on Jack's right answered, "Here and there, no place in particular, maybe down under.

"Australia's sure a long way from here," one man said. No answer was given.

"Want to deal", Jack was asked?

"Why not, and cut for me, too." the stranger on the left added.

So Jack dealt the cards. "OK, high card deals." Jack replied. Each man got a card: one a nine of diamonds, then four clubs, next jack of hearts, then king of diamonds. Jack got an eight of hearts, and the stranger on his right drew an ace of spades. Looking at Jack's card and the stranger said, "Aces and Eights, dead man's hand. That's the tale of Wild Bill Hickock . . . he was holding Aces and Eights when the other man shot him . The stranger started shuffling the cards and Jack's mind traveled at full speed; I must win big; I must win big. What the hell am I doing here?

The cards were placed toward Jack to cut and as he reached for the deck, the hand of the stranger to his left moved over the cards and made the cut. All was acceptable and the deal began.

Everyone anted up ten dollars and all the players put their money to the center of the table, or as they call it, in the pot. First card dealt was face down, and each peeked at their own as it was received. Jack had a seven of diamonds and he opened on a hunch for pot limit. The stranger on his left called; next one raised ten dollars and the next two called. The dealer decided just to call. The next card to Jack was an eight of diamonds dealt face up; one of the men got a jack of clubs and bet ten dollars, all called the bet, even when the dealer raised ten dollars on what he called the come. (The cards will come as expected?)

The next card was dealt and Jack got a six of diamonds, the

stranger on his left now had a pair of fours. He bet ten dollars and when the dealer got his card, he had a pair of nines and bet fifty dollars; the other men started murmuring, a pair of nines showing, must have three to bet like that. The other man had a pair of fours, could have had three . . . Two players dropped out, with two more cards to go.

The next card was dealt and Jack got a five of diamonds. All eyes were on him and the dealer announced, "Workings of a straight flush". The stranger on his left got another four, another player dropped out. Possible four of a kind or a working full house? As cards were dealt, the dealer got a third nine. Possibly four nines or working full house. What hands! The dealer bet the pot limit, Jack must call as he was up to his neck in the betting and must go to the finish...Like it or not. He would lose. The impact of all he would lose became clear...his money, his family, no way to repay Old Howard, and possibly his life. Summing up the stranger's words when he sat down in the game... "Dead Man's Hand"...The last card was dealt and as it started to settle down at Jack's front, it seemed to just float across his other cards and land on the floor at his feet, face down. Jack was sure he saw red diamonds as it floated by...the eerie silence was broken as one of the men watching the game declared, "That card is dead!"

The dealer replied, "I prefer to deal another card." Dealer's choice. The stranger to Jack's left said, "It's a perfectly good card and he should be allowed to keep it."

There was argument from spectators and some ex-players. Was the card good? The owner requested the rule book and searched but found no answers. The dealer insisted it was a dead card. The stranger on Jack's left argued again, "It's good." And to Jack, "Reach down and pick it up if you want it or elect another card."

"Dealer's choice," the dealer announced. "Take a new card." The dealer started to draw another card and the stranger on Jack's left stopped him. "Let the man pick up the card or request another in its place. Dealer's choice was called after

the game started, not before where we could have accepted or rejected. Remember? So come now, let us reason together - let Jack make his decision, and turning from the stranger looked directly into Jack's eyes. His soft gaze and relaxed manner allowed Jack to have a clear mind in his decision.

"I'll take the card dealt," Jack said and reached down to grab the card. But as he did, he was electrified with fear at what he saw. The feet of the dealer were not as ours; in fact, they were not feet at all .. they were hooves? As Jack turned to his left he saw the feet of the stranger who had interceded for him all along and they were a soft rose colored with bronzed lacing of flat sandals wrapped around them. All the promises Jack had made flashed rapidly in sequence, the gambling, drinking, arguing, promises to Old Howard. This time his promise was in the form of a prayer. If granted, he would dedicate the remainder of his life doing what the Lord would expect of him; and he would never break this promise...this one last time request.

All eyes were on Jack as he sat up with the card still facing down in his hand. He placed it on the table in front of him; the men watching asked him to turn it over. When the dealer reached for the card, the stranger on Jack's left stopped him with a softly spoken, "He can do it for himself."

Jack turned the card over to find a nine of diamonds. The dealer stiffened, looked at the stranger on Jack's left. Jack passed the last bet to the stranger on the left. The stranger just called. The dealer bet what he had in front of him, and Jack called the bet, while the stranger on the left scanned both faces, Jack's and the dealer's, then slowly folded his hand, threw the cards to the center of the table and asked Jack, "Have you got it?"

Jack's reply, "Yes I have, if ever I got it, I have it now."

The commotion of the unturned first card had the hall in an uproar, as Jack turned over his hand showing his seven of diamonds...a straight flush.

In the excitement of picking up and partially counting money and trying to respond to the well wishes of the men, it

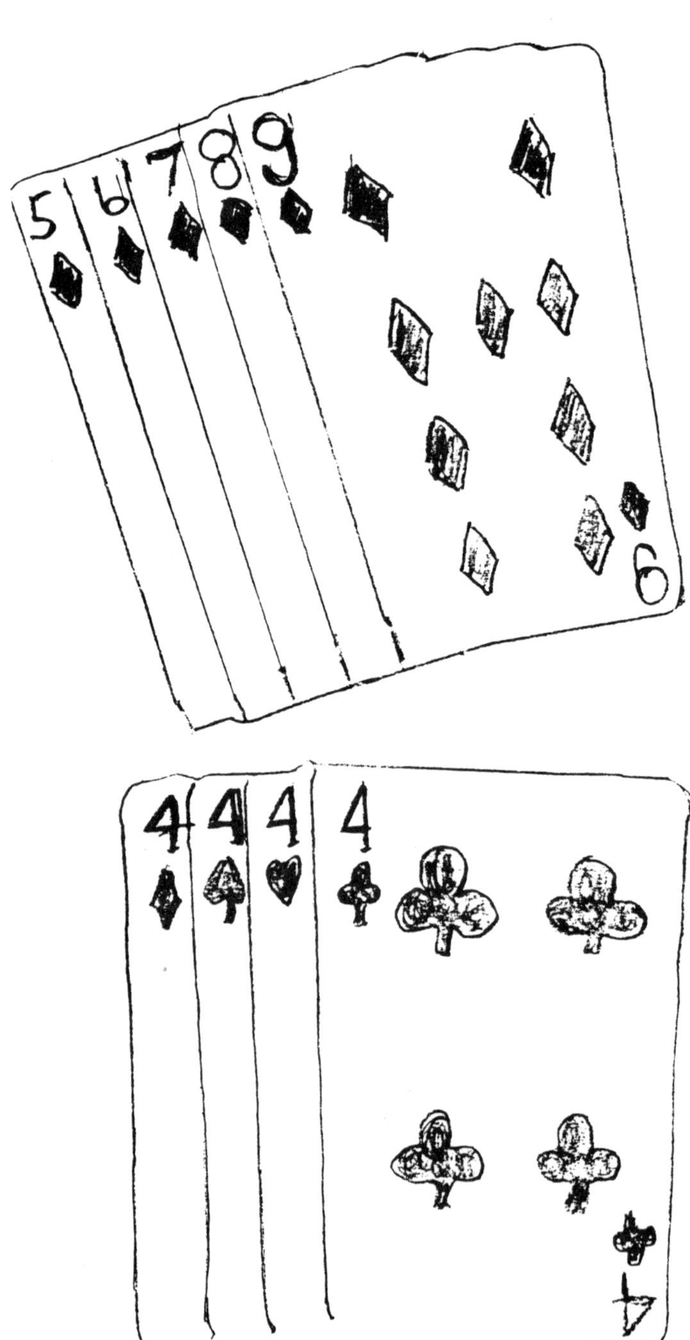

seemed that the strangers had somehow gotten out of sight. Jack's curiosity tempted him to peek at the hand the stranger was holding, when he threw it in. There were four fours. His puzzlement is short lived.

"Where are the two who were here a moment ago, someone asks?" No one seemed to know. Jack was now going to keep his promise, yet he must make one stop on the way home. To Old Howard, to thank him for his help and to return what he had given him.

Susan was delighted at the way Jack was planning to pay the hospital and continue with good plans for their future and for the record, no more of the gambling and drinking. She later called Old Howard to thank him for whatever he did to help and was puzzled by Old Howard's reply. She said "I thought you had?" Silence. She replies, "I don't know, I only see he is a different person now." She hangs up the phone, speaking out loud to no one in particuar, "Old Howard swears, he never contacted anyone, and had no idea what had happened other than he would chat with us tomorrow, as he has guests and they just had set down to talk and enjoy a snack before his friends continue their journey.

Back at the hall, the men were still talking to themselves of the night's happenings, when one of them suggested they look in the restroom or somewhere for the two strangers and as the search continued, one of them who had gone outside, called all the others to show what he had found. A silence came over all of the men as they could not believe their eyes. There in the snow were two sets of prints. One as a person with a flat shoe making the footprint, while the other as a set of hooves, leaving their unmistakable print in the snow, with both going along together for a short length of space then one set going to the left and the other to the right and then just disappearing altogether. Very few men returned to the hall, as most went to their homes at that time.

The magic of the evening was far from over, as the hospital called to inform Jack and Susan their son was going to be

alright and they could pick him up in the morning. As puzzled as the doctors were, every test showed no existing problem remained. It was most certainly a pleasure to give this type of a report over any others and they were all so delighted.

Time has passed and they have a happy family. And, oh yes, Jack kept his word from that night on.

OH, MAN

Oh, Man, in your mold of clay,
What excuse for war do you use today?
Just who offended that stiff neck of yours?
That bombs are prepared,
And your army's sent on long tours.
Oh, Man, in your mold of clay,
Must you bring more horror and fear?
How many more children, do you kill today?
Must you destroy, all we hold dear?
Oh, Man, in your mold of clay,
Stop this self-destruction, this mad journey.
Reach out to each other, in an honorable way.
Time to ask forgiveness, on bended knee.
Oh, Man, in your mold of clay,
Rebuild the future, in complete harmony.
Oh, Man, in your mold of clay,
Do not waste another precious day.
Oh, Man! Oh, Man!
Make peace eternal . . . Make it today.

Notes